Cornerstones of Freedom

The Story of

THE BATTLE FOR IWO JIMA

By R. Conrad Stein

Illustrated by Len W. Meents

CHILDRENS PRESS, CHICAGO

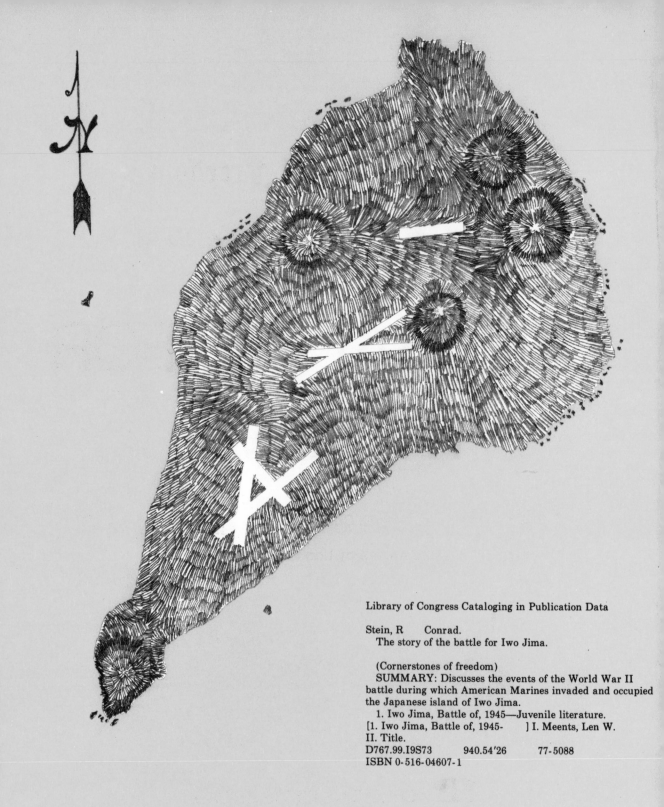

Library of Congress Cataloging in Publication Data

Stein, R   Conrad.
    The story of the battle for Iwo Jima.

    (Cornerstones of freedom)
    SUMMARY: Discusses the events of the World War II
battle during which American Marines invaded and occupied
the Japanese island of Iwo Jima.
    1. Iwo Jima, Battle of, 1945—Juvenile literature.
[1. Iwo Jima, Battle of, 1945-   ] I. Meents, Len W.
II. Title.
D767.99.I9S73   940.54′26   77-5088
ISBN 0-516-04607-1

Mount Suribachi is Iwo Jima. Like the back of an enormous sea turtle, the mountain looms upward from the narrow stem of this island shaped like a pork chop. Iwo Jima is sandy, treeless, and hopelessly ugly. Yet, in February, 1945, many thousands of young Americans and young Japanese were about to die in a battle over this gloomy little rock of an island that no one would ever want to visit, much less live on. Wars are strange that way.

Iwo's only importance was its location. The tiny Japanese-owned island was 660 miles south of Tokyo. It lay midway between the mainland of Japan and the American B-29 bases on Saipan. On the fat portion of the island were two precious airstrips. If the United States held Iwo, P-51 Mustang fighters taking off from the airstrips could escort the big bombers on their raids against Japan. Also, damaged B-29s could make emergency landings on the island. The Americans had to invade Iwo, and the Japanese knew it.

At sunrise on February 19, 1945, guns roared from American ships. Seven giant battleships and dozens of cruisers and destroyers poured shell after shell onto the tiny island. Mount Suribachi, an ancient volcano, looked as if it were erupting again. The shelling was lifted only to allow scores of carrier-based planes to pound the island with rockets and bombs. When the planes left, the big ships opened fire again —until it seemed that Iwo Jima would sink under the weight of shells.

Deep in a cave on Iwo Jima General Kuribayashi wrote a letter to his oldest son while heavy shells exploded outside. The Americans had been bombing and shelling Iwo for weeks, and he had grown accustomed to the constant din of explosions. The letter he was writing was almost a duplicate of one he had mailed months ago. He urged his son to take the father's place and keep the family spirits high. He did not mind giving the same advice as he had in his earlier letter, for he was sure that this one would never be delivered.

Suddenly an explosion from a heavy shell thundered directly outside the General's cave. The ground beneath him shook and rocks and dirt from the roof of the cave fell down on him. The General threw his pen to the ground and pressed his hands over his ears. Agonizing seconds passed. Finally the cave stopped quivering and the noise of the explosion faded into the thunder of more distant explosions.

General Kuribayashi searched through the dirt trying to find his half-written letter. He

could not find it and soon gave up his search. It would only end up in the pocket of some American Marine, he thought.

The General sat in his dark cave thinking about the once-mighty empire of Japan. Four years earlier Japan had had a proud fleet and a well-trained and well-equipped air force and army. Now most of the fleet had been sunk. Japan's airplanes had been shot from the sky, and the army was short of ammunition and food.

Iwo Jima was one of the last outposts of the empire of Japan. The General commanded twenty thousand men, all of whom were prepared to die on this sandy little island. There would be no retreat and no surrender.

"We must all fight until death," General Kuribayashi ordered his soldiers. "Let every man's position be his tomb."

Fighting until death was not a new order in the Japanese Army. Suicidal struggle had long been an important strategy for the Japanese military. Since boyhood, Japanese soldiers had been taught the code of *bushido:* To die in battle for the Emperor was an honor that would be rewarded in heaven; individual life on this earth was unimportant; the survival of Japan, and the spiritual life a warrior would gain after death, were all that mattered; death in battle was glorious, and surrender to the enemy was an unthinkable disgrace.

Troops like the Japanese, who are not afraid to die, can make a powerful army if used correctly. But in earlier battles, Japanese willingness to die actually helped the Americans. Japanese officers waving swords and shouting their fearsome cry, *"Banzai!"* would lead their men in hopeless suicidal charges against American positions. Often the Americans had only to wait for these charges so they could cut down the Japanese with superior firepower.

On Iwo Jima General Kuribayashi would not change the strategy of suicide, only the tactics. He ordered that no officer lead his troops on a wild charge. Instead they were told to stay in their caves and fortified positions and fire at the enemy from there. This tactic would force the Marines into close combat, and then the Japanese could attack with rifles and grenades. Japanese men would die, but the General hoped that each of his soldiers would take several of the enemy with him.

Iwo Jima was a perfect site for General Kuribayashi's battle plan. Hundreds of natural caves dotted the island, and Mount Suribachi was a beehive of them. In addition to the caves, the Japanese built pillboxes to defend the airfields. Pillboxes are concrete bunkers with holes in the walls for firing guns, machine guns, and rifles. They were cleverly camouflaged and built so strongly they could be knocked out only by a direct hit from a big gun on a battleship.

In landing ships off the beaches at Iwo Jima American Marines of the Third, Fourth, and Fifth Divisions waited for the invasion. They knew the Japanese were always tough opponents. But they did not realize they were facing an enemy so well dug in and so willing to die. Iwo would become the bloodiest battle of the Pacific war.

The morning of February 19 was perfect for an amphibious invasion. The sky was cloudless and the sea smooth. Marine General Holland Smith peered at the island through binoculars from the command ship. Because of his quick temper he was nicknamed "Howlin' Mad" Smith. But today he felt worried, not angry. This was the landing he feared the most. The night before he had hoped something would happen to cancel the operation. He was certain of victory but feared that casualties at Iwo would be the worst in the history of the Marine Corps.

The young Marines waiting to make the assault were confident and full of fight. All were secretly afraid, but covered their fear with assuring chatter. "They always save the tough ones for the Marines," one said. "Yeah, we always go in first," answered another.

The Marines are a special service, and they believe they are the best fighting men in all the United States forces. Other services were jealous of the publicity Marines received in the newspapers back home. A standard army joke held that a newspaper photographer was assigned to each Marine rifle squad. As the Marines waited in the lower decks of LSTs (landing ship tanks), one sailor called down to them, "Go get 'em, you glory hounds."

At nine in the morning, five thousand yards off the beach at Iwo Jima, the first line of flat-bottomed LSTs lowered their ramps. As soon as the ramps dropped, small tanklike floating vehicles called "amphtracs" splashed out of the LSTs and into the water. One correspondent wrote that it looked "like all the cats in the world having kittens."

Pushed on by their tanklike treads, the amph-tracs crawled through the water toward the beach. Each one carried about twenty Marines. The amphtracs moved toward the island in a straight line, as if they were on parade.

A Japanese soldier hidden behind some rocks on Mount Suribachi looked down at the lines of amphtracs heading toward the beach. The slow amphtracs would make easy targets, he thought, but General Kuribayashi had forbidden Japanese gunners to fire on landing craft. Such fire would only expose Japanese guns to the big guns of the American Navy. The Japanese General's plan was to let the Marines land on the beach and then destroy them with hidden guns. Next the Japanese soldier thought about how casual the Americans seemed to be, even though they were on the verge of battle. He saw an American destroyer cruising in the waters not five hundred yards from him. He could hear popular music being played from radios on the destroyer and he could see U.S. sailors leaning over the rail of their ship. Their shirts were off, and they looked at the island as if they were tourists. Strange people, these Americans, the Japanese soldier thought.

The amphtracs bumped against the beach and, driven by their caterpillar treads, climbed a few feet to dry land. They stopped, rear ramps dropped, and Marines laden with heavy packs poured out. The Americans discovered that Iwo Jima was covered with a surface of volcanic ash as soft as newly fallen snow, and they sank up to their ankles with every step. Most had to crawl on their hands and knees to get a few yards off the beach. The Pacific sun rose swiftly and the Marines were soon drenched in sweat.

In the first few minutes no shot was fired at the Marines. Had the Japanese abandoned Iwo? Could it be possible that naval gunfire had killed them all?

But Japanese guns were not silent for long. Suddenly the Marines were hit by artillery, mortars, and machine guns. The fire came from every hidden corner of the island. The Marines looked for cover, a hole to dive into, a fallen tree to hide under. There was none; only the soft sand and volcanic ash. The desperate men pressed themselves into the sand, hoping that somehow the earth would swallow them up.

One young Marine heard a blast and felt himself being lifted upward. In midair he turned over with his back pointed toward the ground. It

seemed as if he would never return to earth again. He felt strangely embarrassed. Everyone on the beach could see him hanging in the air like a fool. Finally he crashed on the soft sand, landing on his heavy pack. He tried to roll over but could not. Now he felt helpless, like a mud turtle turned over on its shell waving his arms and legs uselessly in the air. When he finally turned over, he checked himself, but could find neither blood nor broken bones. A miracle. A shell had blown up in the ground beneath him and he had survived without a scratch.

A half hour after the first wave of Marines landed, larger landing ships delivered tanks to the beaches. The tanks slid in the sand like cars caught in snow. Unable to advance, the tanks were easy targets for Japanese guns. A painful message became clear to the men on the beach. Tanks would not be effective on this island, nor had naval gunfire knocked out the Japanese positions. This battle would have to be won by the riflemen.

By twilight, thirty thousand Marines had landed on Iwo. They huddled together on a narrow strip of beach measuring three miles long and about half a mile wide at its deepest point. That first night was a nightmare. Hour after hour Japanese fire poured into Marine landing zones. Wounded and dying men crowded into aid stations set up on the beach. Many wounded men, unable to crawl to the aid stations, were alone on the beach. In between shell bursts, their desperate cries could be heard, pleading for the Navy medics to come and help them. "Corpsman. Corpsman, over here. I'm hit. I'm hit bad."

At dawn, a group of Marines who were crowded together on the beach had a visitor. A black and white fox terrier dog had suddenly joined their ranks. No one knew whether he had belonged to the Japanese or had come ashore with one of the Marines. At first the Marines called to him, but they scattered when they discovered the fox terrier had found a plaything. In his mouth the dog held a live hand grenade. He dropped the grenade on the ground and stood yelping. One Marine threw a stick, hoping to divert the dog's attention. When the dog chased the stick the Marine stepped gingerly toward the grenade. But the dog playfully rushed back and picked up the grenade again. As the Marine scrambled away the dog chased after him, wanting to drop the grenade at the man's feet. Finally the Marine managed to separate the dog from the grenade long enough to disarm the grenade, and the battle for Iwo Jima continued.

According to plans the Fifth Marine Division started an advance toward the base of Mount Suribachi. The Fourth Division moved to the right to try to capture the airfields. The Third

Division was held in temporary reserve, and would land the next day.

From far out at sea battleships lobbed shells over the Marines' heads and onto Japanese positions. Destroyers crept as close to the beach as possible to lend supporting fire. Now ground observers could direct the fire from the big ships, and shells began hitting even the smallest targets. More tanks landed, and this time harder ground was found so the tanks could push inland.

Still, the brunt of the battle fell on the riflemen. The Japanese, brave and disciplined, clung to their position and fired at the Americans. The Marines, tough and aggressive, attacked with bayonets, knives, and the little shovels called entrenching tools that they carried on their packs. On Mount Suribachi, Japanese soldiers who had run out of ammunition rolled boulders down on advancing Marines. The year was 1945, but some of the fighting on Iwo was like combat waged between Stone Age tribes in the years before history was written.

Wherever possible, flamethrowers were used to burn the Japanese out of their pillboxes. Flamethrowers are the most gruesome weapons in the arsenal of the infantryman, but they are effective. Flamethrowers shot flame onto the pillboxes near the airfields. Then Marines pushed dynamite into the gun holes of the pillboxes. Yard by yard this incredibly bloody battle continued.

Marine General Holland Smith visited aid stations on the beaches. He was shocked. At first he could not believe the sight of the mangled bodies he saw strewn in front of him, and he hoped that reports of the enormous number of Marine dead were exaggerated. But General Smith's worst fears had come true. Iwo Jima was going to become the most costly battle in the history of the Marine Corps. He felt like weeping, but there was no time. His duty was to continue the battle.

In a cave somewhere on the island, General Kuribayashi continued his battle plans. Most of his telephones had been knocked out, so he had to use runners to keep in touch with his units. Like General Smith, he was shocked by the number of men he had lost in just two days, but still he urged his men to fight until death. He, too, had a duty to perform.

On the nearby island of Chichi Jima, a group of Japanese planes carrying one bomb each roared off an airstrip. Chichi Jima, like Iwo Jima, had been heavily bombed, but these planes were expertly camouflaged and had escaped damage. They flew in a pattern designed to escape the constantly patroling American fight-

ers. Their targets were the big ships supporting the operation. Each Japanese pilot hoped to crash his plane into an American carrier.

These were suicide pilots, known as *kamikazes*. They were named after a mysterious wind that destroyed a Mongolian fleet that was about to invade Japan in the twelfth century. The Japanese believed the wind that destroyed the invading fleet had come from the breath of God. *Kamikaze* in Japanese means "divine wind." The Japanese hoped that these twentieth century *kamikazes* would again save their empire from an invading force.

It was almost dark when the *kamikazes* spotted the American carrier *Saratoga* and dived after her. The carrier's anti-aircraft gunners responded with furious fire. Two of the Japanese aircraft were set on fire, but their dying pilots kept the planes boring in toward the carrier. Some American sailors thought the pilots were already dead and that their ghosts were flying the planes. The two flaming aircraft crashed into the side of the *Saratoga*. Two more suicide planes crashed and exploded on the carrier. Another plane launched a bomb that tore through the flight deck of the big ship and exploded inside. The *Saratoga*, burning wildly, was towed away from Iwo Jima with 123 of her crew dead.

The light carrier *Bismarck Sea* was not as lucky as the *Saratoga* had been. Hit by a single *kamikaze*, she burned for three hours before rolling over and sinking. She lost 218 of her men.

After three days of bitter fighting on Iwo, units of the Fifth Marine Division struggled up Mount Suribachi. It seemed that every rock on the mountain was a secret lair for a Japanese soldier. Some sniped at the Marines with rifles. Others launched mortar shells at them. Still other Japanese charged at the advancing Marines with grenades in their hands; each was resolved to blow himself up, but hoped to take four or five of the enemy with him.

Finally a group of exhausted Marines reached the top of Mount Suribachi. Thousands of Japanese, full of fight, remained on the island, but the Marines had finally reached Iwo's highest point. A Marine lieutenant had a flag tucked inside his shirt. Someone found a pole, and soon the American flag fluttered on top of the mountain.

Men at the base of Mount Suribachi cheered. Destroyers close enough to see the flag blasted their whistles. One sailor on a destroyer, although awed by the Marines' performance on Iwo, still grumbled, "Look at those Hollywood Marines."

A Marine Colonel who saw the flag thought it was too small. He wanted everyone on the island to be able to see the American flag waving proudly over Mount Suribachi. He ordered a larger flag and a longer pole to be taken from an LST and delivered to the top of the mountain.

When the larger flag arrived, several photographers milled about suggesting different poses. Joe Rosenthal, a photographer for the Associated Press, was drenched in sweat as

he aimed his camera at the men raising the flag. Rosenthal, a chubby man, looked out of place beside the slim young Marines. Six Marines started to raise the flag and the sweating photographer snapped a picture as the pole was halfway up. He thought it was a pretty good shot and sent the negative back to a ship to be developed and wired to the United States. Rosenthal had no idea he had just taken the most famous picture of the war.

Even though the flag was flying over Mount Suribachi, the battle had not yet been won. The Japanese still fought and died for every foot of the island. The Marines saw many days of bloody fighting before this battle ended. But, day after day, the Japanese resistance weakened, and those who remained alive were quickly running out of ammunition and food.

Heavy equipment was soon on the beach and American Seabees readied the captured airstrips for the fighters and bombers. Often the Seabees drove their bulldozers and graders while Japanese riflemen sniped at them from the hills. Just thirteen days after the invasion, while the battle still raged, a B-29 with damaged fuel tanks crash landed at Iwo. The fuel tanks were repaired and the B-29 took off again, the crew eternally grateful to the Marine Corps.

Before the end of the war more than two thousand B-29s used Iwo Jima for emergency landings. The island also became a vital base for fighters that escorted the big bombers to and from Japan. There is no doubt that the capture of Iwo Jima saved American lives, but at a terrible cost. More than five thousand Marines lost their lives on Iwo, and more than seventeen thousand others suffered wounds.

On March 16, 1945, after almost four weeks of constant combat, the island was declared occupied by the United States and the battle was officially over. General Holland Smith, exhausted and saddened by the casualties, said only, "This was the toughest yet."

Although the battle was "officially" over, General Kuribayashi and about three thousand of his men were alive and hiding in the caves that dotted the island. On March 27, the General emerged from his cave a broken man. He had lost almost twenty thousand fine young men on this little island. He knew the American victory at Iwo Jima meant the final defeat of Japan. The General bowed north toward Japan, mumbled a few words, and killed himself by thrusting a sword through his stomach.

Many of his officers followed their General and committed suicide. Others rounded up what Japanese soldiers they could find and led the men in one last screaming *banzai* charge. These desperate attackers were wiped out to a man at little loss to American forces.

Even so, hundreds of Japanese remained and lived miserable lives in the caves of Iwo Jima. Like stray cats, they came out at night to try to steal food from the Americans. The atomic bomb was dropped on Japan and the war ended, yet they stayed in their positions as General Kuribayashi had ordered. As the months passed, many finally surrendered, others died of illness, but still others held out, ashamed to face the disgrace of surrender.

In 1951, six years after the end of the war, the last two known Japanese soldiers on Iwo Jima crawled out of their cave and gave themselves up. Later, one of them returned to the island with a television crew to do a news show for Japanese TV. As the former soldier showed the television crew a cave near a cliff, some old reminder of death and duty must have pushed into his thoughts. Suddenly he ran toward the edge of the cliff. As the shocked TV crew watched, he leaped over the side, shouting something, possibly *banzai*, and dived to his death.

When the fighting had wound down on Iwo, the barren little island looked uglier than ever. Shell holes pocketed the ground, making it look as lifeless as the moon. Someone commented that Iwo looked "like hell with the fire put out."

A battle fought as desperately as the Battle of Iwo Jima always produces many heroes. Seven Marines fighting on Iwo won the highest award the nation can give, the Congressional Medal of Honor. Admiral Nimitz, naval commander for the operation, believed that all the men who served on the island were heroes. He wrote, "Among the Americans who served on Iwo Jima uncommon valor was a common virtue."

The Japanese also fought bravely, but the losing side is rarely given the opportunity to honor its heroes.

News of the battle at Iwo Jima had made the headlines in U.S. newspapers every day for at least two weeks. In many ways World War II was more than a war for the United States. It was a national adventure, almost a crusade. The American public loved heroes, and the Marines provided them by the dozen.

Rosenthal's photograph of the second flag raising at Mount Suribachi arrived in the United States in time to make the Sunday papers. Newspapers all over the country placed the dramatic photo on the front pages. No combat photo taken anywhere at any time during the war thrilled the public more than the shot taken on top of Mount Suribachi.

After the war, the photo inspired the bronze monument to the Marine Corps in Washington, D.C. The huge statue was sculpted by Felix de Welden, and dedicated by President Eisenhower on November 10, 1954—the 179th birthday of the United States Marine Corps. Inscribed on the marble base are the words of Admiral Nimitz: UNCOMMON VALOR WAS A COMMON VIRTUE. The imposing statue overlooks the Potomac River near the Arlington National Cemetery.

On Iwo Jima today, cool winds creep off the sea and blow among the sand and volcanic ash. The winds meet at the center of the island and create little whirlpools of dust that dance about the surface like ghosts. The once vitally important airstrips are now half buried in sand. Near the unused airstrips are graveyards where crosses and stars stand in unending rows like wooden soldiers standing at attention.

Iwo Jima is still a gloomy little rock of an island that no one would even want to visit, much less live on. Yet thousands of men died in a furious battle for this tiny, ugly bit of the earth. Wars are strange that way.